Colorful
Lateral
Thinking
Puzzles

Paul Sloane and Des MacHale

Sterling Publishing Co., Inc.
New York

Acknowledgments

Richard Morton Jack for *Flight of Fancy*; Kristina Routh for *The Find*; John Faben for *Foolproof*; Jonas Bernander for *A Famous Swede*; K Lang for *Deafinitely*; Lizzy Rengel for *His Own Fault*; Torgeir Apeland for *Orient Express*; Michael Hong for *Break-in*; and Ann Sloane for *What a Drag*.

Library of Congress Cataloging-in-Publication Data

Sloane, Paul, 1950-
Colorful lateral thinking puzzles / by Paul Sloane and Des MacHale.
        p.   cm.
    Includes index.
    ISBN 0-8069-9392-8
    1. Lateral thinking puzzles. [1. Lateral thinking puzzles. 2. Puzzles.]
    I. MacHale, Des. II. Title
GV1507.L37 S55 2004
793.73—dc22   2003 025212

10   9   8   7   6   5

Edited by Nancy E. Sherman

Published by Sterling Publishing Co., Inc.
387 Park Avenue South, New York, NY 10016
© 2003 by Paul Sloane and Des MacHale
Distributed in Canada by Sterling Publishing
c/o Canadian Manda Group, 165 Dufferin Street,
Toronto, Ontario, Canada M6K 3H6
Distributed in the United Kingdom by GMC Distribution Services,
Castle Place, 166 High Street, Lewes, East Sussex, England BN7 1XU
Distributed in Australia by Capricorn Link (Australia) Pty. Ltd.
P.O. Box 704, Windsor, NSW 2756, Australia

Sterling ISBN 0-8069-9392-8

For information about custom editions, special sales, premium and corporate purchases, please contact Sterling Special Sales Department at 800-805-5489 or specialsales @sterlingpub.com.

Contents

Introduction

How many different ways can you look at a tree? You can look up from the ground, down from the crown, out along its branches, or from a great distance away. You can see it in summer all covered in leaves or in winter, denuded and bare. You can focus on it so tightly that you lose sight of the forest or you can lose sight of the tree among thousands of others in a blazing fall panorama. Just as there are ways without number to look at a tree, there are numberless ways to look at a problem.

When you take just one view, it limits your ability to assess a situation or to solve a problem. Each new perspective yields further information. Lateral thinking involves taking a different approach, which can lead to more creative solutions. If you had been given the project to design a better computer keyboard, what would you have done? Would you have looked at a keyboard and tried to make it better? Or would you have looked at the way people use keyboards and then come up with the idea of a mouse?

Let these puzzles encourage you to approach situations from new directions. They are most effective when used by a group, with one person knowing the answer and the others asking questions. The person who knows the solution can answer questions only yes or no. Those who ask the questions have to gather a great deal of information. They have to try different lines of attack. They have to test their assumptions, use their imaginations, and think laterally. They have to find the answer given in the book.

In real life, these same skills help generate alternatives. Typically, real-life problems have a number of potential solutions; another, better one is always possible. Surely, something far better than a computer mouse is just waiting to be invented!

Puzzles

On the Right Track

Clues, p. 40, Answer, p. 85

Two men were on the run from the police, who tracked them to the edge of a seaside cliff. The police found two sets of tracks leading to the cliff edge and none leading back. The shoe sizes of the men were different and it was clear that the footprints had been stepped in only once. So the police deduced that the men had leapt into the sea. But they were wrong. What had happened?

The Scratched Man

Clues, p. 41, Answer, p. 93

A man was found dead on a small island in the middle of a lake. All the police could find was a little scratch on his cheek. No one else had been on the island all day. How did the man die?

Clean Sweep

Clues, p. 41, Answer, p. 72

He would not have died if the chef had been neater.

The Banal Canal
Clues, p. 40, Answer, p. 90

Why did a company dig a canal joining two very minor and unimportant tributaries of the Mississippi River?

Pushing the Envelope
Clues, p. 40, Answer, p. 88

A man received a letter, correctly addressed. He did not recognize the writing or the envelope; nevertheless, he knew who had sent it before he opened it. How?

Further Bother with the Other Brother
Clues, p. 40, Answer, p. 78

John said to Tim, his older brother, "You are stronger than I am, but I can put something into the wheelbarrow and wheel it to the apple tree that I'll bet you can't wheel back." Tim took the bet and lost. What was it that John wheeled to the apple tree?

Leader of the Pack
Clues, p. 41, Answer, p. 81

Why did the people of the tribe choose an animal as their leader?

Game, Set, Match
Clues, p. 41, Answer, p. 78

John mixed some chemicals with a stick and then used the stick to make a mark on the floor. What everyday thing did he thus invent?

Hole in One

Clues, p. 41, Answer, p. 79

Why did a man cut a hole in his mattress?

Accidental Death

Clues, p. 42, Answer, p. 68

The town council introduced measures designed to reduce traffic accidents. Why did they lead to more deaths?

Rolling Stone

Clues, p. 42, Answer, p. 88

A stone was found bearing writing in ancient Greek, concerning gifts given by a king. Why is this stone now considered to be one of the most important archaeological finds of all time?

The Forgotten Drink

Clues, p. 42, Answer, p. 77

A mother called her son in from the back porch where he was having a soft drink. He came in and went to bed. Why were many children pleased that he forgot to bring in his drink?

Not Today, Thanks

Clues, p. 42, Answer, p. 84

A man drove every day from his hometown to the town where he worked. One fine day he found he could not enter the town where he worked. Why not?

Putt Out

Clues, p. 44, Answer, p. 88

A golfer died because he holed a putt. How come?

One Stormy Night...

Clues, p. 43, Answer, p. 85

This is a moral dilemma that has been used as part of a job interview:

You are driving along in your two-seater car on a wild, stormy night. You pass a bus stop where you see three people waiting for the bus:

   a) An old lady who looks as if she is about to die.

   b) An old friend who once saved your life.

   c) The perfect man (or woman) you have longed to meet.

Knowing that there is room for only one passenger in your car, what would you do?

An Irish Invention

Clues, p. 43, Answer, p. 68

The British stop it at 10. The Americans continue it to 17. An Irishman invented it. What is it?

Deadly Return

Clues, p. 43, Answer, p. 73

A man died because he went home too quickly. How come?

The Church Tower

Clues, p. 43, Answer, p. 72

A young man went off to war. He returned some time later. When he saw the church tower near his home, he knew that his family was in serious trouble. Why?

Money Maker

Clues, p. 44, Answer, p. 83

A man walked into a store and bought some candy. He and the clerk did not know each other. He paid with a $20 bill and received $21 in change. Why?

What a Drag

Clues, p. 44, Answer, p. 95

Why was a woman pulling three heavy old tires through the park?

Lighting Up Time

Clues, p. 44, Answer, p. 81

A man lived alone. Every night he went upstairs, turned the light on, and then went to bed. In the morning he turned the light off. Why?

Seals on Strike

Clues, p. 42, Answer, p. 88

The seals were the star attraction at the water park and played to packed houses. One day they refused to perform. Why?

The Monarch's Secret

Clues, p. 44, Answer, p. 93

What unusual security device did the Queen of England use when giving the royal assent to secret cabinet papers?

Better Off Robbed

Clues, p. 45, Answer, p. 69

A woman was better off because she was robbed. How come?

Beach Party

Clues, p. 45, Answer, p. 69

Some sailors decided to cook a meal on a sandy beach. They put their pots on some alkali they used for embalming and the unexpected result was something we use every day. What is it?

Money Is the Root of All Evil

Clues, p. 45, Answer, p. 83

A man took $10,000 in cash to the bank. He and the money were never seen again. Why?

It's a Steal

Clues, p. 45, Answer, p. 80

Why did a man use his cell phone to report a theft that did not take place?

Ignorance Is Bliss

Clues, p. 46, Answer, p. 80

The man who made it did a brilliant job. The man to whom he gave it agreed, but he did not want to keep it. So he gave it to someone who did not know what it was. What was it?

The Find

Clues, p. 46, Answer, p. 91

When Augusta found the money, she cried. Why?

Boxed In

Clues, p. 46, Answer, p. 70

A man is sitting in a room. A woman enters, carrying a closed box. They do not know each other and neither says a word. How does the man know what is in the box?

Freeze Wheeze

Clues, p. 45, Answer, p. 77

Why did the director on a movie set order a bucket of ice cubes to be delivered during filming?

The Queen's Mistake

Clues, p. 47, Answer, p. 93

The Russian was sent to England to correct the Queen's mistake. He succeeded. What was the Queen's mistake?

Open Door Policy

Clues, p. 49, Answer, p. 85

He escaped death because the door was open. How?

Dig Deep

Clues, p. 49, Answer, p. 73

Why did a man bring a bag of earth into a hospital?

On the Wrong Track
Clues, p. 47, Answer, p. 85

After several train crashes, the British rail authorities considered investing in a new technology that would improve safety by ensuring that trains did not go through red lights. A safety expert then pointed out that this plan would probably lead to more fatalities. How come?

Mark Up and Up and Up
Clues, p. 48, Answer, p. 82

Which commonly consumed commodity has the greatest mark-up in price from the cost of raw material to the price paid by the consumer? It is not gasoline, cocaine, CDs, truffles, or pearls. So what is it?

Spot the Dot
Clues, p. 47, Answer, p. 89

When is it not appropriate to put a dot (called a "tittle") over a lower case letter *i*?

Wind-up
Clues, p. 46, Answer, p. 95

A man changed all his clocks to daylight savings time. He did 9 of them at midnight but waited until 8 A.M. the next day to do one other. Why did he wait?

Smart Move
Clues, p. 48, Answer, p. 89

Why would an intelligent, healthy, middle-aged man take up smoking?

Orient Express

Clues, p. 48, Answer, p. 86

A man is sitting in a train. A bandage is covering twelve wounds on the back of his right hand. What happened?

Life's a Gas

Clues, p. 48, Answer, p. 81

A driver runs out of gas. His car tank holds exactly 13 gallons. He walks to the gas station. He has with him three empty unmarked containers with capacities 11 gallons, 6 gallons, and 3 gallons. Using these containers only, how does he bring back exactly 13 gallons with no gas wasted?

Break-in

Clues, p. 47, Answer, p. 70

Joe pressed the doorbell of the house. No one answered. He climbed over the fence and found the window unlocked. The lights were off and the house was dark. He slowly opened the window and entered. He was startled to see a dark figure. Joe reached for his gun with his right hand and the figure reached for a gun with his left hand. Joe took his gun and fired. What happened next?

Diamonds Are for Never

Clues, p. 47, Answer, p. 73

Robbers knew that a woman had some very valuable diamonds. They waited until she was away on holiday and then burgled her house. They searched high and low, but they could not find the diamonds. What had she done with them?

Deafinitely

Clues, p. 50, Answer, p. 73

A deaf man sits in a city bus behind two other men. After several minutes, he's almost sure that one of them is new in town. How does he know?

Upstairs, Downstairs

Clues, p. 50, Answer, p. 94

A man had six clocks in his house. They were all in perfect working order. He checked them all when he went to bed and they all showed the correct time. When he awoke the next morning, the three clocks upstairs in his house all showed 7:30. He immediately went downstairs, where the three clocks all showed exactly 6:55. What was going on?

His Own Fault

Clues, p. 50, Answer, p. 79

If he hadn't stolen the wallet, he would have lived longer.

Dry One

Clues, p. 50, Answer, p. 74

A man was in a boat on the open sea. There was nothing but water for miles around. He stood up in the boat to get a better view, but overbalanced and fell out. When he climbed back into the boat, he was completely dry. Why?

Dry Two

Clues, p. 50, Answer, p. 74

Another man was in another boat on the open sea. There was nothing but water for miles around. He stood up in the boat to get a better view, but overbalanced and fell out. When he climbed back into the boat, he was completely dry. Why?

Legal Eagle

Clues, p. 48, Answer, p. 81

What bird must by law always have exactly fourteen feathers?

The Dog, the Cat, and the Canary

Clues, p. 51, Answer, p. 91

A man came home one day and gave his wife a live, pedigreed terrier as a pet. She was delighted and kept it in her room. The next week he gave his wife a present of a beautiful live Siamese kitten. She was pleased and kept it in her room. The next week he gave his wife a present of a live singing canary. She took the bird and kept it in her room. The dog never chased the cat and the cat never chased the bird. Why not?

West Wing

Clues, p. 50, Answer, p. 95

A couple wrote to the Vice President warning him that the Texas eagle was facing extinction. Why did his reply infuriate them?

No Sight, Excite

Clues, p. 51, Answer, p. 84

A little girl is leading her younger brother down the street. He has his eyes tightly closed but he is excited. Why?

False Note

Clues, p. 51, Answer, p. 75

A woman dies and seems to have left a suicide note. How did the police discover that she was in fact murdered?

I Spy

Clues, p. 51, Answer, p. 79

During WWII, two German agents in London went into a bar, but their cover was quickly blown. How?

Musical Murder?

Clues, p. 51, Answer, p. 83

Howard was a good musician and composer. In recognition of his ability, he was appointed conductor of the City Symphony Orchestra. This allowed him to conduct programs of his works and those of other modern composers. But the members of the orchestra were very traditional and could not play the pieces well. Despite all of Howard's efforts, the violinists came in too soon, the clarinetists were off-key, and the trombonists played too loudly. Howard became angry and frustrated. He seized the trombone from the lead trombonist, whirling it around. It struck the trombonist and the poor man died of a fractured skull. Howard claimed it was an accident, but at his trial several members of the orchestra testified about his fits of anger. He was found guilty of murder and sentenced to death in the electric chair. Howard continued to compose; in fact, he created some of his best works as he waited on death row. As he was taken to the electric chair, he whistled his latest composition. He continued whistling as the circuits were closed and a massive current was applied to him. Amazingly, he survived. Why?

Can-Do Attitude

Clues, p. 52, Answer, p. 71

Who said this, "What I can, I eat, and what I can't, I can?"

The Stranger Who Sang

Clues, p. 53, Answer, p. 94

Peter played in a band that needed a new singer. He was in town one day. He approached a complete stranger and asked him if he had ever sung in a band and whether he would like to do so again. The stranger, who had been completely silent until that moment, said yes to both questions. How did Peter know that the man might be interested?

A Quickie

Clues, p. 55, Answer, p. 67

What is the only day of the week that does not end in a *y*?

False Start

Clues, p. 52, Answer, p. 75

A man arranged his escape from prison. He climbed the wall and found the car that his friend had left for him. The car was in perfect working condition but he could not start it. Why not?

The Ideal Candidate

Clues, p. 52, Answer, p. 92

A man is interviewing people who want to become his body-guard at a huge salary. Part of the job description is that the bodyguard be prepared to risk his life for his boss. The employer observes the candidates in the waiting room through a one-way mirror for some time and immediately chooses a candidate for the job without speaking to any of them. Why?

Cans and Bottles

Clues, p. 52, Answer, p. 71

Every morning before he goes to work, a man lines up three tin cans and three bottles on the wall of his garden. Every evening when he comes home, the tin cans and the bottles are no longer on the wall. What is going on?

A Famous Swede

Clues, p. 52, Answer, p. 67

He is one of the best-known people in Sweden, but he has never done anything special. So what is he known for?

Holy Cow

Clues, p. 54, Answer, p. 79

There was a monorail train system for many years in Ireland on which loads had to be balanced on opposite sides of the car. A lady wanted to transport a piano on the train, so a local farmer lent a cow to balance it. However the cow ultimately had to be returned. How did they solve the problem of getting the cow back?

The Thoughtless Thief

Clues, p. 53, Answer, p. 94

A man goes into a shop. When the shopkeeper turns around, the man grabs something expensive from the counter and runs out of the shop. The shopkeeper has never seen the man before and cannot remember what he looks like. Yet the police arrest the criminal within a few hours. How does this happen?

Flight of Fancy

Clues, p. 53, Answer, p. 76

Why did the king order his troops to catch birds?

Last Breath
Clues, p. 53, Answer, p. 80

A man did not breathe for five minutes, but he did not lose consciousness. Then he died. How?

Shapely Object
Clues, p. 53, Answer, p. 89

What common object contains seven rectangles, a complete circle, two circular segments, and four separate circular quadrants?

Inflation
Clues, p. 54, Answer, p. 80

A few minutes before a man grabs an object, it is worth about $15. When he grabs it, it is worth several hundred thousand dollars. He insists he has every right to grab it, but somebody else grabs it from him and insists that it belongs to *him*. What on earth is it?

Stranded
Clues, p. 56, Answer, p. 90

A man is found dead on a little island—he is the only person on the island. He did not die of starvation, he did not commit suicide, he was not killed by a wild animal, and he did not die of poisoning or thirst. There are no trees on the tiny bare island. How did he die?

Cut It Out
Clues, p. 54, Answer, p. 72

A woman died because of a pair of scissors—but she was not stabbed, nor did she come in contact with the scissors. What happened?

Trapped

Clues, p. 55, Answer, p. 94

In the film *The Sound of Music*, there is a very obvious blunder not noticed by the director. It has to do with fruit. Can you figure out what it is?

Pointless Exercise

Clues, p. 54, Answer, p. 87

Why did a man who did not want to exercise or to meet people join the local gym?

Puppy Love

Clues, p. 55, Answer, p. 87

A woman was out walking her dog when a thief robbed her. Why was she not upset?

The Shine Sign

Clues, p. 55, Answer, p. 94

A shoeshine boy was having a bad business day on the city streets. Then he displayed a simple notice containing just four words, and business began to boom. What did the notice say?

Objective Achieved

Clues, p. 60, Answer, p. 84

A woman puts object A into object B. An hour later, she puts object B into object A. A day later, she puts object B into object C. Finally, she puts object A into object C. What are objects A, B, and C, and what is going on?

Tap, Tap, Tap

Clues, p. 56, Answer, p. 90

A man was driving a car when he heard a tapping. When he investigated, he had a heart attack. Why?

The Helpful Robber

Clues, p. 54, Answer, p. 92

Why was the lady glad he tried to rob her?

Stick with It

Clues, p. 57, Answer, p. 89

A man is preparing to drop a letter into a mailbox in a remote location. When he takes the stamp out of his wallet he notices there is no glue on the back. How does he manage to attach the stamp?

Wheel of Fortune

Clues, p. 56, Answer, p. 95

A woman was found unconscious next to a roulette wheel. What had happened?

The Diver and the Ruler

Clues, p. 56, Answer, p. 91

The diver had to travel further than normal because the ruler wanted something none of his predecessors had had. What was it?

It Won't Wash

Clues, p. 56, Answer, p. 80

Why did a man fill a bathtub with water when he had no intention of taking a bath?

No Room at the Inn

Clues, p. 57, Answer, p. 84

Why does a world-famous hotel always close down during the busiest tourist season of the year?

What Was the Point?

Clues, p. 57, Answer, p. 95

Why did the Romans make their spears so that they broke when they were used?

Ouch, That Hurts!

Clues, p. 57, Answer, p. 86

Why did a woman deliberately trap her hair in a window?

Suddenly Drowning

Clues, p. 57, Answer, p. 90

A man swam confidently for five minutes and then suddenly started to drown. The water conditions did not change and he did not get a cramp. Why did he start to drown?

French Lesson

Clues, p. 60, Answer, p. 77

He became the first man in France ever to be prosecuted for this offense, though many people have done it. He thought he was just doing his job. What did he do?

Church Bells

Clues, p. 58, Answer, p. 71

Why did a man deliberately set off his cell phone in church?

Stone Me

Clues, p. 55, Answer, p. 89

Why was a man arrested for having a pebble in his pocket?

Stir the Porridge

Clues, p. 58, Answer, p. 89

A man who had committed no crimes and had no criminal record went to prison. He was forced to stay there. Why?

Move One Digit

Clues, p. 59, Answer, p. 83

Make this equation correct by moving one digit and nothing else: $62 - 63 = 1$.

Drop Dead Gorgeous

Clues, p. 59, Answer, p. 73

A little girl took part in a fancy dress competition and as a result, her father died. How come?

Bare Necessities

Clues, p. 59, Answer, p. 69

A man stripped naked and many people's lives were saved. How?

The Headless Nails

Clues, p. 59, Answer, p. 92

If only they had had some headless nails, they could have changed the course of history. How?

Eyes Wide Shut

Clues, p. 60, Answer, p. 75

Normally you should drive with both eyes open because you have better depth perception that way. When is it recommended that you drive with one eye open and one eye closed?

Close Family

Clues, p. 60, Answer, p. 72

A woman says, "My daughter's sister is also my sister." How can this be true?

Gender Bender

Clues, p. 60, Answer, p. 78

What word changes from masculine to feminine and from plural to singular when you add an *s* to it?

Terse Verse

Clues, p. 61, Answer, p. 90

A famous singer plans to perform a song at her next concert, but she does not bother to learn the words to the first verse. Why not?

Next, Please

Clues, p. 61, Answer, p. 83

A man is traveling when he sees this sequence: E...5...1. He knows what will come next. What is it?

Ape in a Scrape

Clues, p. 62, Answer, p. 68

A naturalist was observing a monkey that belonged to an endangered species when he saw its life being threatened. He did not do anything to protect it. Why not?

Fishing Expedition

Clues, p. 65, Answer, p. 76

Why did a man take a fishing line into a laundry?

A Tale of a Tail

Clues, p. 61, Answer, p. 67

A woman driving on a major boulevard suspects that the man in the car behind her is following her and may attack her. However, she does not wish to call the police in case she is mistaken. How does she find out if he is following her?

Perception of Deception

Clues, p. 59, Answer, p. 86

Why did a child pretend to be a vegetarian when he was not?

Number Stumper

Clues, p. 61, Answer, p. 84

If you take a 3-digit number and place the first digit between the second digit and the third, you can produce something we all use practically every day. What on earth is it?

Road to Perdition

Clues, p. 63, Answer, p. 88

Why was a road built that led nowhere?

Absent Without Leave

Clues, p. 63, Answer, p. 67

A man told a real estate agent the type of house and location he wanted. The agent recommended a house and the man bought it. When he moved in he was disappointed because a feature he expected was absent. But the real estate agent had not lied. What was the feature?

Coat Conundrum

Clues, p. 61, Answer, p. 72

Why does a man use a heavy woolen coat as a coat all summer and then put it away all winter?

Two Lefts Don't Make a Right

Clues, p. 62, Answer, p. 94

A man leaves home, makes three left turns, and returns home without speaking to anyone. He is very pleased. Why?

The Extra Shoe

Clues, p. 62, Answer, p. 91

Why did a man take three shoes with him to a meeting, and who was he?

The Kangaroo and the Emu

Clues, p. 62, Answer, p. 92

The Australian cricket team badge (and the Australian coat of arms) features a kangaroo and an emu. These creatures share an unusual characteristic that embodies the spirit of the team. What is it?

No Reference Point

Clues, p. 62, Answer, p. 83

A man who had been a model worker with a firm for many years asked for a reference so that he could apply for a new job. However, his boss in the old job, who liked him but had no desire to keep him, refused to give him a reference. Why?

Foolproof

Clues, p. 63, Answer, p. 76

Bob wrote a story. He died. Sharon read the story. Her husband died. The story was never read again. Why not?

Heavyweight Champ

Clues, p. 63, Answer, p. 79

A woman manages to win a race even though she is heavily weighed down. How?

Reversal of Fortune

Clues, p. 63, Answer, p. 88

After the war, the direction of flow in a piece of commercial equipment was temporarily but deliberately reversed. Why?

Elem Entry

Clues, p. 64, Answer, p. 74

A robber prowls among apartments in a big complex. Vulnerable people, like old ladies living alone, are warned by the police not to answer knocks or doorbells in case it is the prowler. However, he seems to have no difficulty getting into such people's apartments. How does he do it?

Life begins...

Clues, p. 64, Answer, p. 81

What is unique about the number 40?

Beginner's Luck

Clues, p. 65, Answer, p. 69

A man who was a poor and inexperienced poker player sat down to play poker with several other men who were all skilled and experienced players. The man won a lot of money. How?

Loss Leader

Clues, p. 64, Answer, p. 81

A man wrote a book with a particular aim in mind. When it was published, he immediately realized that he had failed. Why?

Plane Speaking

Clues, p. 64, Answer, p. 86

The designers of the B-17 bomber pared back the weight of the aircraft to what they felt was the absolute minimum, but a child suggested how it might be further reduced. What did he suggest?

Objectionable Object

Clues, p. 64, Answer, p. 84

Some people love it, others hate it. It is used for just a few seconds and then can never be used again. It changes the appearance of people who have already taken great care with their appearance. What is it?

The **WALLY** Test

Now that you have warmed up with the lateral thinking puzzles, you are ready to try your wits on the official World Association for Laughter, Learning, and Youth (WALLY) Test. Get a pencil and paper. You must answer each question immediately after reading it. You have one minute to complete the test and you are not allowed to change any answer once it is written. Do not look at the solutions until you have answered all the questions.

1. What should you do if a tiger eats your pencil?

2. Why did the golfer wear two pairs of trousers?

3. What always comes at the end of Christmas Day?

4. What kind of water never freezes?

5. How many legs does a horse have if you call its tail a leg?

6. Forward I am weighty, backward I am not. What am I?

See WALLY test solutions on page 71.

Clues

On the Right Track

- The two men had approached the edge of the cliff.
- The tracks were true and had not been tampered with.

Further Bother with the Other Brother

- What John wheeled to the apple tree was not particularly heavy, but it was impossible for Tim to wheel it back.
- John could wheel it back.
- So could most other people, but not Tim.

The Banal Canal

- The answer involves a boat.
- Digging the canal allowed the company to make more profit.
- It enabled the company to do something that it was previously not allowed to do.

Pushing the Envelope

- He did not know the contents of the envelope.
- He received many letters but this one was different.
- There was nothing special about the stamp, envelope, writing, or general appearance of the envelope.

The Scratched Man

- The man had been murdered.
- No guns, arrows, darts, spears, or knives were involved.
- He and his murderer had shared a common interest.

Clean Sweep

- A man died accidentally in a restaurant.
- He did not die from any hygiene-related issue.
- His instructions were not followed.

Hole in One

- He lay on the bed on his back, but he did not sleep there.
- He cut the hole to deceive people.
- He put a part of his body through the hole.

Leader of the Pack

- They did this when they were in trouble.
- It was not symbolic or religious.
- The animal had an ability that they needed.

Game, Set, Match

- He was surprised at what happened.
- The chemicals on the stick reacted when he scratched the stick on the floor.
- He invented something that nearly everyone uses at some time.

Seals on Strike

• The seals swam one circuit underwater and then went back to their pen and would not come out.

• They were fine healthy animals and there was nothing unusual about the day or the time.

• It is thought they were scared.

• They had seen something.

Accidental Death

• The town council wanted to slow down traffic in certain places.

• They installed speed bumps—bumps in the road.

• Some vehicles kill people; other vehicles save people.

Rolling Stone

• The stone solved a mystery that had baffled scholars for years.

• The stone enabled the writings of a whole civilization to be understood.

• The stone has a place of pride in the British Museum in London but many people in Egypt would like to see it there.

The Forgotten Drink

• This happened in 1905.

• He had stirred his drink with a stick.

• He accidentally created something that became very popular.

Not Today, Thanks

• Weather was not a factor and there was no accident.

• He did not meet anybody and nobody stopped him.

- He should have known that on this particular day he could not get into the town.

One Stormy Night...

- If you ignore your old friend you appear disloyal. If you neglect to help the old woman you appear uncaring. If you ignore the person of your dreams, it might show you are lacking in courage and ambition.
- How can you meet all these needs and impress the interviewers?

An Irish Invention

- It does not involve time, money, weights, or distances.
- It is something that you have heard of but probably never used.
- The higher the number the more trouble there is.

Deadly Return

- If he had returned more slowly, he would have survived.
- He did not use a vehicle and there was no fire or traffic accident.
- There were no other people or animals in his home.
- He did not drown but water is involved.

The Church Tower

- He was very surprised to see the church tower.
- The tower was not damaged and did not show any writing, signs, or decorations.
- It was normally hidden from view.
- His family were farmers.

Money Maker

- There was no wrongdoing or criminal activity.
- The clerk gave the correct change.
- The man was on vacation.

What a Drag

- She did not want the tires for any purpose other than to drag across the park.
- She did it many times backwards and forwards.
- She wore a harness with ropes attached to the old tires.

Lighting Up Time

- He turned the light on for a specific reason concerning safety.
- He was not afraid of animals, criminals, or other people.
- He very rarely had visitors.

The Monarch's Secret

- Queen Victoria wanted to ensure that no unauthorized person could tell what she had communicated in the cabinet papers.
- She read the cabinet papers, sometimes made comments, and then signed them.
- The cabinet papers were transported to and from the Queen in a completely secure manner.

Putt Out

- The golfer was thrilled to sink the putt.
- There were other people watching and he acknowledged their applause.

- He was killed in a tragic accident.
- If he had missed the putt, he would have lived, but someone else might have died.

Better Off Robbed

- A man stole her purse and her credit cards.
- He used the credit cards to buy something.
- He succeeded but the result was not what he expected.

Beach Party

- The heat fused the sand and the alkali to make a new material.
- What they discovered helps us see the world in new ways.

Money Is the Root of All Evil

- If he had not gone to the bank, he would not have died.
- His death was accidental—there was no criminal activity involved.
- He drowned.

It's a Steal

- He called the police to say that he had seen a shop being broken into. He was lying.
- He did it for personal gain—but there was no money involved.
- He phoned from his car.

Freeze Wheeze

- It was nothing to do with food or drink.

- It concerned an effect he wanted to achieve in the film.
- The actors disapproved.
- He was filming at a different time of year from that in which the story was set.

Ignorance Is Bliss

- All three are healthy men.
- The third man would be unhappy if he knew what he had.
- Criminal activity is involved.

Wind-up

- The man had time to do all his clocks at once.
- One clock was different from the others.

The Find

- Augusta was a normal, healthy woman.
- It was her own money she found.
- She cried because she was unhappy.
- Finding the money confirmed her fears.

Boxed In

- There are no markings on the box and it is a regular cardboard box.
- There is nothing unusual about the woman.
- The place they meet is not relevant.
- If he had been blind, he would still have known what was in the box.
- He does not see, smell, touch, hear, or feel what is in the box.

The Queen's Mistake

- The queen was Queen Victoria.
- Her mistake was a matter of diplomatic protocol.
- It involved a town on the border of England and Scotland.
- The mistake endured for 100 years but no great damage was done.

On the Wrong Track

- The technology would work well and stop trains going through red lights.
- There would be fewer train accidents.
- To install the new equipment would involve significant costs and delays.
- An unforeseen consequence would lead to more fatalities.

Spot the Dot

- It would be ingenuous to give a direct clue for this puzzle.

Break-in

- Fortunately, no one was injured.
- Joe's actions were a poor reflection on him.

Diamonds Are for Never

- She hid the diamonds in the house.
- She put the diamonds in a place where they were hard to see.

Mark Up and Up and Up

- It is a food.
- It is cooked.
- It is a popular snack.

Smart Move

- He found cigarettes unpleasant and distasteful but he forced himself to smoke them.
- No bets, tests, dares, or wagers were involved.
- He took up smoking for financial advantage.

Open Door Policy

- He was in prison.
- He did not escape from the prison.
- The door was opened and then closed. During that period he did not leave his cell, but he escaped death.
- Some of those with their cell doors closed, died.

Orient Express

- The man was not alone.
- He had three friends.
- They were responsible for his injuries.
- Hunger had been the motivation.

Life's a Gas

- He is not a mathematical expert.
- He performs the task easily.
- He does not pour from one container into another.

Legal Eagle

- The bird is a cock.
- It is not alive.
- Men and women sometimes strike this bird.

Dig Deep

- It was not used for a medical purpose.
- But it was used during a medical procedure.
- He was planning for the future.

Upstairs, Downstairs

- The clocks were not all the same type.
- If the clocks downstairs had been upstairs and vice versa, it would have made no difference what appeared on them in the morning.

Deafinitely

- The deaf man observed the two other men.
- By their actions, he could tell that one was new in town.
- Being on the bus is relevant.

His Own Fault

- The man was a criminal.
- He died because he stole a wallet.
- He died following a car accident.

Dry One

- The man was alone in a small boat.
- He fell out of the boat but did not fall in the water.

Dry Two

- There were many other people in the boat.
- The boat was cruising in the Caribbean.
- He fell out of the boat but did not fall in the water.

West Wing

- They wrote to the Vice President of the United States.
- He wrote a polite and concerned reply.
- He was concerned about the preservation of wildlife.

No Sight, Excite

- They both have good eyesight and are in perfect health.
- He has his eyes closed but not for any medical reason.
- On their way home they both have their eyes open.

False Note

- She apparently wrote a note to a friend saying she was going to end it all.
- The police examined the note carefully.
- It was impossible to tell if it was her hand that had written the note.

I Spy

- They ordered two drinks.
- The barman asked about the nature of the drinks.
- They gave themselves away.

Musical Murder?

- There was a reason why the current would not flow through him.
- The whistling was not relevant.
- Howard was very bad at something.

The Dog, the Cat, and the Canary

- All the pets were alive and very active, with good sight and hearing.
- The dog would have chased the cat, had it seen the cat. The cat would have chased the bird, had it seen the bird.
- When his wife took the bird to her room, it was her only room.

Can-Do Attitude

- He was a businessman.
- He dealt in a food product.

A Famous Swede

- There is nothing special about his appearance, physical attributes, or achievements.
- He is disliked.
- People feel sorry for him.
- He is known for something he did not do.

False Start

- The man was experienced with cars and driving.
- The car worked exactly as intended.
- Someone else could have started it.

The Ideal Candidate

- He does not recognize or hear any of the men.
- He uses logic to figure out which man might risk his life.
- His choice is not based on strength, size, scars, color, race, or general physical appearance.
- He observes what they do while they are waiting.

Cans and Bottles

- The man is not a criminal.
- The location of his house is important.
- He does it for material gain.

Flight of Fancy

- It was not to eat or train the birds.
- He wanted to let them go so that they would return to their nests.
- There was a military purpose.

The Stranger Who Sang

- Peter did not recognize the man.
- The man had been standing still.
- The man had been reading.

Last Breath

- He died a violent death.
- He did not have any special physical abilities or characteristics.
- Water was not involved.
- He was fully conscious during the five minutes when he did not breathe.

Shapely Object

- It is large.
- It is usually green, but not always.
- If you don't figure this out, you should kick yourself!

The Thoughtless Thief

- The man stole a camera.
- That was not his purpose when he entered the shop.
- After the theft, there were developments in the case.

Inflation

- There was financial gain involved, but no criminals.
- The man had gone out for entertainment with no intention of acquiring anything.
- This incident was caught on television and became the subject of a court case.

The Helpful Robber

- The woman had been wronged.
- The man thought he would have an easy robbery.
- He rescued her instead.

Pointless Exercise

- The man went to the gym, but did not use any of the exercise equipment.
- He did not speak to anyone at the gym.
- He wanted to improve his house.
- His actions were beneficial to him and to those around him.

Holy Cow

- The cow was returned on the monorail.
- Whatever balanced the cow would have to be returned as well.
- The farmers there had many cows.

Cut It Out

- Someone else used the scissors to cut something and she died as a result.

- No strings or ropes are involved.
- She was asleep at the time.

A Quickie

- It is the day we all look forward to.

Puppy Love

- The thief stole her bag.
- The bag was empty when she set out on the walk.
- The bag was not empty when the thief stole it.

The Shine Sign

- The sign was intriguing.
- The shoeshine boy made an offer.

Stone Me

- The man was breaking the law but most people would not consider him a criminal.
- He did not have any particular use in mind for the pebble.
- He took it as a souvenir.

Trapped

- The mistake is an anachronism—it could not have happened at that time.
- It involves a box of citrus fruit.
- The fruit came from the Middle East.

It Won't Wash

- There was nothing wrong with the bathtub and he was not testing it.
- He was doing another job that required the bathtub to be full.
- He did not use the water in the bathtub.

The Diver and the Ruler

- The diver was a man diving for pleasure.
- The ruler lived in the Middle East.
- The diver had no contact with the ruler and was not a threat to him.
- The ruler normally lived in the capital of the country.

Tap, Tap, Tap

- The man was a criminal.
- The tapping was real but it was not caused by the engine or any mechanical part of the car.
- He had stolen the car.

Wheel of Fortune

- She was vain.
- A man had advised the woman to bet on a certain number.
- She had bet on another number.

Stranded

- He was the only person on the island.
- He expected to be safe there.

- He was killed violently.

No Room at the Inn

- The hotel caters mainly to tourists.
- It has to close during the busiest season for practical reasons.
- It is world famous for one unique attribute.

What Was the Point?

- The spears were used to throw at enemies.
- The heads of the Romans' spears were designed so that they broke off on impact.
- This was to help protect the Roman soldiers.

Stick with It

- He uses something else that is sticky.
- He could be in the desert or the forest and still do this.
- He uses what he has.

Ouch, That Hurts!

- She trapped the hair on her head—not cut hair.
- She was alone at the time. No one else was involved.
- She did it for reasons of safety.

Suddenly Drowning

- Something changed, but it was nothing to do with the water.
- At times he was a very good swimmer; at other times he could not swim.
- He was not normal.

Stir the Porridge

- He was not a prison guard or official.
- He was visiting an inmate.
- He did something wrong.

Church Bells

- He was not being disrespectful.
- The cell phone played a particular tune.
- The phone was used as a substitute.

Perception of Deception

- The child came from a poor family.
- He was not trying to avoid anything.
- He was trying to gain something.
- This happened in Europe.

Move One Digit

- The end result still equals 1.
- Use your powers of lateral thinking.

Drop Dead Gorgeous

- She wanted to dress as a bride.
- She lived in Asia.
- She took something to make her costume.

Bare Necessities

- This has nothing to do with experiments, medicine, or war.
- The people were traveling.
- He averted a disaster.

The Headless Nails

- The headless nails were needed for a specific purpose, but not to attach anything.
- This occurred during a time of war.
- A headless nail cannot be extracted.
- A little man had to go to a different island.

French Lesson

- He was charged with a criminal offense.
- He used a weapon but no one was hurt.
- He was a shepherd.

Objective Achieved

- The objects are all containers.
- She bought the first object in a shop and that is where it went into the second object.
- When the second object was no longer needed, it went into the first object.
- Eventually the first object was no longer needed.

Close Family

- Adoption is involved.
- The woman's daughter's natural sister was the woman's adopted sister.
- A natural mother and daughter are involved and two natural sisters are involved.

Eyes Wide Shut

- It is recommended that you drive with one eye open and one eye closed during certain circumstances to improve safety.
- By closing one eye, you protect it.

Gender Bender

- You add the *s* at the end of the word.

- It starts as a plural ending in *s* and ends as a singular ending with *ss*.

Terse Verse

- She is professional and diligent.
- The performance goes well.

Next, Please

- The man is traveling vertically.
- The symbols are shown on an electronic display.
- No particular mathematical or language skills are involved.

A Tale of a Tail

- She continues driving toward her destination.
- She undertakes a maneuver to check whether the car behind is following her.

Number Stumper

- You start with a number and end with a symbol.
- The symbol is related to the original number.
- The number is 100.

Coat Conundrum

- It is an old coat.
- He does not wear the coat.
- It is used for deception.
- This is a long-standing practice.

Two Lefts Don't Make a Right

- He knows as soon as he leaves home that he has achieved his objective.
- He wears a uniform.
- His home is not a house.

Ape in a Scrape

- The naturalist could have acted to protect the monkey but he did not do so.
- Danger to himself was not a consideration.
- He was facing a moral dilemma.

The Extra Shoe

- He wore two of the shoes.
- He feigned great anger.
- He was a famous political leader.

The Kangaroo and the Emu

- The kangaroo and the emu share a characteristic that has more to do with obstinacy than courage.
- They share a physical inability.

No Reference Point

- The man wanted a reference and his boss would have liked to give him one.
- He was prevented by company policy.
- It was a government agency.

Foolproof

- Bob was a brilliant writer.
- Bob was murdered.
- Sharon's husband was murdered.

Heavyweight Champ

- Everyone in the race was weighed down.
- Anyone not weighed down would be at a disadvantage in this race.
- Although it is over a short distance, most of us could not compete in this race.

Reversal of Fortune

- The equipment normally carried a fluid in one direction only.
- It was temporarily used to carry a different fluid in the opposite direction.
- This was done to help avert a disaster.

Absent Without Leave

- The feature of the property was not something inside the house or garden.
- It had to do with the location.
- There was a beautiful lake by the house.

Road to Perdition

- People were very reluctant to drive down this road even though it was perfectly safe to do so.
- This happened in the United States.
- The road was considered unlucky.

Elem Entry

- The robber deceived the old ladies into opening their doors.
- He did not pretend to be someone else.
- He did not ring their doorbells.
- He exploited their kindliness.

Loss Leader

- The author's manuscript was perfect. It contained only that which it was meant to contain.
- His publisher added the author's name to the book.
- The book had had a particular characteristic, which was now ruined.

Plane Speaking

- The child did not suggest that any equipment be removed from the plane.
- He suggested a change to the plane's appearance.

Objectionable Object

- It is used on special occasions only.
- People throw it.
- Everyone laughs—except the person who has to sweep it up.

Life begins...

- This is not a mathematical property.
- Forty is different from all other numbers.
- It has to do with order.

Fishing Expedition

- The laundry was open to the public.
- It contained coin-operated washers and dryers.
- He was a criminal.

Beginner's Luck

- The man had no special powers or abilities that helped him at playing cards.
- The other men suffered from no disadvantages or disabilities that prevented their playing well.
- The man had never met the other players before but he had been invited to join their game.

The Advanced WALLY Test

Before you tackle the next section, let's see what you have learned. Get a pencil and paper. You have one minute to complete this advanced WALLY test and you are not allowed to change any answer once it is written. Do not look at the solutions until you have answered all the questions.

1. What can be found in the center of Latvia?

2. Can you name three consecutive days without using the words Monday, Wednesday, or Friday?

3. What is the longest word in the English language?

4. You are in a race and overtake the person who is in second place. What place are you now in?

5. You are in a race and overtake the person who is in last place. What place are you now in?

6. A murderer is condemned to death. He has to choose between three rooms. The first is full of raging fires, the second is full of assassins with loaded guns, and the third is full of lions that haven't eaten in three years. Which room is safest for him?

See advanced WALLY test solutions on page 75.

Answers

A Famous Swede

He is Christer Pettersson, a drug addict who was accused of the murder of Olof Palme, the Swedish prime minister who was assassinated in 1986. He was found guilty but was acquitted on appeal. So he did not do anything remarkable but, because of his trial and appeal, his name is very well known.

A Quickie

Tomorrow.

A Tale of a Tail

She takes four right turns and finds herself back on the same road going in the original direction. When she sees that the car is still behind her, she knows she is being followed.

Absent Without Leave

The real estate agent told him the house was only fifteen minutes away from where he was going to work. This was true in winter, when the man bought the house, because the huge lake in front of it was frozen solid. In summer it took nearly an hour to drive around the lake.

Accidental Death

The town council had speed bumps installed on the roads in order to slow down traffic and thereby reduce accidents. Unfortunately, all the ambulances in the town had been fitted with hydraulic lifts to help lift disabled passengers. These lifts grounded on the speed bumps. Many ambulances were damaged and the rest could not be used on streets with the bumps. Fewer ambulances and longer trips meant that more accident victims died before reaching the hospital. This true story demonstrates the law of unintended consequences.

An Irish Invention

It is the Beaufort scale of wind forces.

Ape in a Scrape

A rare leopard that was also an endangered species was stalking the monkey. The naturalist decided it was best to let nature take its course.

The Banal Canal

The company wanted to open a casino on its property but state laws were very restrictive regarding gambling. They took advantage of an old law that allowed gambling on steamboats on the Mississippi River and its tributaries by creating their own tributary on their land.

Bare Necessities

In India, a man wearing only a loincloth was walking along a lonely railroad track when he noticed a rail had slipped out of place. There was a train approaching, so he stripped off his loincloth and waved it furiously to warn the train driver. The train stopped and many people were saved.

Beach Party

These ancient Phoenician sailors had stumbled onto the discovery of glass.

Beginner's Luck

The man was a politician who had been bribed by several unscrupulous businessmen into giving them planning permission for a lucrative development contract. The problem was how to pay him without arousing suspicion. They invited him to play poker with them, and then deliberately lost. If they drew a good hand they folded, and if they had a weak hand they bet heavily against him. There is no law saying you must try hard to win at poker, so they were able to transfer the money to him under cover of the card game.

Better Off Robbed

The thief placed a bet on a horse using the woman's credit card and the horse won. The luckless thief did not realize that the winnings would be automatically credited to the woman's credit card account.

Boxed In

The man is allergic to cats and feels the allergy symptoms coming on, so he knows the box contains a cat.

Break-in

The mirror shattered.

Can-Do Attitude

The speaker was someone whose business was canning food —in this case, a fish cannery.

Cans and Bottles

This happened during WWII in Europe, when many things were in short supply. The man's garden wall backed onto a railway line near a station. As the steam trains pulled slowly past the wall, the train drivers and guards would throw lumps of coal at the cans and bottles to try and knock them over. The man collected the lumps of coal for fuel.

WALLY Test Answers

Total up your correct answers. Then see where you fit on this table:

Score	Official Rating
5–6	Smart Aleck
3–4	Wally
0–2	Mega Wally

1. Use a pen!
2. In case he got a hole in one!
3. The letter y.
4. Hot water.
5. Four. Calling the tail a leg does not make it one.
6. A ton.

Church Bells

The man set off his cell phone at a wedding ceremony in the church because the organist failed to show up and the man's cell phone was programmed to play the wedding march.

The Church Tower

The church had been submerged many years earlier when a dam was built to create a reservoir. The fact that he could see the church tower meant that the reservoir was at a very low level and the country was suffering a terrible drought. His family were farmers and he knew that all their crops would be ruined.

Clean Sweep

A man with a serious allergy to nuts gave very careful instructions at his local restaurant. They had to prepare his beef curry according to a precise recipe that contained no nuts or seeds whatever. One day there was a new chef who was given the recipe; unfortunately, he smudged it with sauce. He made the curry the way he always did—with peanut sauce, which killed the diner.

Close Family

The woman and her mother had each adopted one of a pair of sisters.

Coat Conundrum

He is a farmer who uses the coat on a scarecrow in spring and summer to keep the birds away from his seeds and plants.

Cut It Out

The woman was asleep on her water bed when a prankster punctured the bed with the scissors. Unfortunately, the water flooded her bedside TV set and she was electrocuted.

Deadly Return

The man lived on a boat and one day he went scuba diving. Sadly, he returned from the deep too quickly and died of the "bends," a painful and deadly effect of quick decompression.

Deafinitely

The deaf man sees that as one man talks to the other, he points his finger at a number of shops, landmarks, theaters, and restaurants as they pass. He deduces that one man is showing the city to the other.

Diamonds Are for Never

She froze each diamond in a separate section of a tray of ice cubes, where they were very hard to see.

Dig Deep

You can play cricket for Yorkshire only if you are born on Yorkshire soil. A man was very anxious that his son qualify to play cricket for Yorkshire and planned to move his wife there from London for the baby's delivery. However, his wife went into labor prematurely and was rushed to a maternity hospital. The man placed a sterilized bag of Yorkshire soil under the delivery table and so could say quite correctly that his son was born on Yorkshire soil.

Drop Dead Gorgeous

In the Far East, the girl cut a square from her father's mosquito netting to make a veil for her costume. As a result her father was bitten and died of malaria.

Dry One

The boat bumped into an ice floe. The man fell out of the boat and onto the ice.

Dry Two

The man was a stowaway in a lifeboat on a ship. He fell out of the lifeboat into the ship.

Elem Entry

The robber recorded the sound of a cat meowing in distress. He played this outside their doors and old ladies were deceived into opening the door for him.

Eyes Wide Shut

When you are driving at night and the lights of an oncoming car temporarily blind you, it is best to close one eye so that you will be blinded in one eye only.

False Note

The note was an e-mail sent from the woman's PC. However, the police noticed that it was sent after the time she was known to have died.

Advanced WALLY Test Answers

Total up your correct answers. Then see where you fit on this table:

Score	Official Rating
5–6	Smart Aleck
3–4	Wally
0–2	Mega Wally

1. A TV.
2. Yesterday, today, and tomorrow.
3. Smiles—there is a mile between the first letter and the last.
4. You are in second place.
5. You cannot overtake the person in last place. You would have to be behind him.
6. Lions that have not eaten for three years are dead.

False Start

This happened early in the 1900s. Before the man went to prison, all cars used crank handles to start the engine. He had been in prison for 10 years, during which time electric starters were made standard on all cars. He searched in vain for a way to crank start the engine and never tried turning the key.

Fishing Expedition

He attached the fishing line to a $20 bill and fed it into the change machine. He collected the change and then reeled the note back out. He repeated this until the change machine was empty. He was spotted on the surveillance camera and arrested.

Flight of Fancy

This story is from *King Harald's Saga,* which chronicles the life of Harald, the last Viking warrior. Before becoming king of Norway, he fought as a mercenary for the Byzantine Empire. Commanded by Harald, the Greek king's forces were besieging a town in Sicily that was well provisioned and able to withstand a long siege. He ordered his men to catch small birds that nested under the eaves in the townspeople's dwellings and flew out each day in search of food. Once he had collected a large number of them, he had wood shavings smeared with wax attached to their backs. These were set alight and the birds released. The birds immediately flew back to their nests under the villagers' thatched roofs. Thus they started many small fires and soon the whole town was ablaze. The people surrendered. Harald spared them and took control of the town.

Foolproof

Bob wrote a murder mystery called *Foolproof.* He was right;

the murder plot was 100% foolproof. He submitted it to Sharon, his editor. Sharon was astounded; it was brilliant. She could get rid of her husband, and no one would suspect a thing. There was just one hitch; Bob would know that she had done it. She would have to dispose of Bob. Sharon killed Bob in the foolproof manner outlined in his story. She then killed her husband. Of course, then she had to dispose of the manuscript—as good as the story was, she could hardly publish the method of her crimes.

Forgotten Drink

In the cold night, the drink froze around the stick he had used to stir it. It was 1905 and 11-year-old Frank Epperson had just invented the Popsicle®.

Freeze Wheeze

This happened on the set of the movie *The Wicker Man.* The scene was set in early May, but it was shot on a freezing day in October. The actors' breaths kept condensing on contact with the cold air, producing visible little clouds of moisture. The director insisted that each actor suck on an ice cube to cool his or her breath so that it did not produce telltale clouds of moisture and give away the actual conditions during filming.

French Lesson

Herve Bernardon was a shepherd in the Hautes Alpes region of France. He killed a wolf that had been preying on his sheep. Wolves had been exterminated in France in the 1920s but had started to reappear from Italy in the late 1990s. They are now a protected species.

Further Bother with the Other Brother

John took his brother in the wheelbarrow.

Game, Set, Match

When he scraped the stick across the floor, it burst into flame. It was 1827 and John Walker, an Englishman, had invented matches.

Gender Bender

Princes becomes princess.

Heavyweight Champ

The race was held underwater in Polynesia, and the contestants were held down with weights. Holding their breath, they "ran" a course of 60 meters marked out with pegs.

His Own Fault

A man steals a wallet. Soon after, he is knocked down as he crosses the street. When he is brought to the hospital, he is unconscious and has lost a lot of blood. The doctors open his wallet to see who he is. They find a card stating that for religious reasons he does not want blood transfusions or organ transplants.

Hole in One

He was an actor in a TV series, playing the part of a man in a hospital who had had his lower leg blown off in an accident. He lay on the bed on his back with his right leg bent at the knee, the lower part of his leg stuck through the hole, and was therefore hidden.

Holy Cow

At the other end of the line, they borrowed two fine fat twin calves to balance the cow. Then on the return journey, the calves balanced each other.

I Spy

One of the Germans ordered two martinis. The barman asked, "Dry?" Dry sounds exactly like the German word for three, *drei*. The German automatically replied, "*Nein, zwei,*" meaning, "No, two."

Ignorance Is Bliss

Counterfeit money.

Inflation

The man was at a baseball game when a player hit a homerun. The ball flew into the crowd and the man grabbed it, but in the melee, he lost it and someone else picked it up. The homerun represented a record number by a hitter in one season and the ball was therefore a valuable piece of baseball memorabilia. A judge decided that the ball should be sold and the money divided between the two men. (Barry Bonds of the San Francisco Giants was the hitter; it was his 72nd season homer.)

It's a Steal

He was speeding and a police car pulled him over. Before the policeman reached his car, he quickly called to report a robbery at a shop nearby. The policeman was summoned by his dispatcher to the supposed crime, thus letting the villain go free. (Cell phone records helped catch him later.)

It Won't Wash

The man was installing tiles in the bathroom. The new bathtub was plastic and moved slightly when filled with water. He filled the tub with water to see where it lined up with the tile when full. This way, he could extend the grouting to the very edge of the bathtub and it would not crack or leave a gap when the tub was full.

Last Breath

He fell out of an airplane at over 30,000 feet. The force of the air against him made him unable to breathe out, but that did not matter. During free fall, air diffuses through the skin, making normal breathing unnecessary, so he was doing fine. Until he hit the ground.

Leader of the Pack

The tribe were Bedouins, nomads who live in the desert. When they cannot find water, they let a camel lead them, as camels are better able to find water.

Legal Eagle

It is a shuttlecock as used in badminton—it was originally a real bird, of course.

Life begins...

Forty is the only number whose letters are in alphabetical order.

Life's a Gas

He measures 11 gallons into the biggest container and 2 gallons into either of the others. The gas station pump records the exact amount dispensed.

Lighting Up Time

He was a lighthouse keeper.

Loss Leader

Ernest Vincent Wright wrote *Gadsby*, a book of over 50,000 words, among none of which occurred the most common letter in the English language, *e*. However a careless printer put the author's name on the title page. Since the name contained three *e*'s, it rather spoiled the effect.

Mark Up and Up and Up

Surprisingly, the answer is popcorn, which has a 5000% mark-up in the cinema.

Money Is the Root of All Evil

The man took the money to the riverbank, where he slipped, fell in, drowned, and was washed out to sea.

Money Maker

An American on vacation in Canada paid with a US $20 bill and was given $21 Canadian in change.

Move One Digit

$2^6 - 63 = 1$

Musical Murder?

Howard was a good musician but a very bad conductor!

Next, Please

The man is going down in an elevator while looking in the mirror. He sees the reflection of the floor numbers 3, 2, 1, and knows that he will arrive at the ground floor next and the display will show G.

No Reference Point

He worked for the British Secret Service. As part of their security policy, they do not publicly admit that they exist, that they have employees, or what the employees do.

No Room at the Inn

This hotel in Sweden is made entirely of ice and is open during the winter. In summer, it melts and is therefore closed in August, when most Swedes are on holiday.

No Sight, Excite

They are going to the cinema together, but they are late and they know the show has already started. Guided by his sister, he has his eyes closed so that when they get inside, he will be able to see in the dark and lead them to two empty seats.

Not Today, Thanks

The place where he worked was in a different country and the border was closed for a national holiday. The man was Jordanian and he worked in Israel. The Israeli border closes for Yom Kippur.

Number Stumper

If you take the number 100 and move the symbols as directed, you get the percentage symbol—%.

Objectionable Object

It is confetti.

Objective Achieved

The woman bought a new waste paper basket (A), which she put into a paper bag (B). When she got home, she put the paper bag (B) into her new waste paper basket (A), and later into her garbage can (C). Years later she will put the waste-basket into the garbage can.

On the Right Track

One man carried the other to the cliff edge. The other man then carried the first backwards, away from the cliff edge. This left just two tracks, both heading toward the cliff and stepped in once only.

On the Wrong Track

The cost of this new system would mean a cutback on the number of trains running. With fewer trains, more people will take to the roads, where the death rate is much higher.

One Stormy Night...

One candidate out of 100 gave what was judged the best answer. He simply answered, "I would give the car keys to my old friend, and let him take the lady to the hospital. I would stay behind and wait for the bus with the woman of my dreams."

Open Door Policy

Thomas Payne, the author and philosopher, was imprisoned in France soon after the Revolution. Those selected for execution the next day had an X marked on the door of their cells. Payne's door opened outwards and was wide open. So the guard marked the X on the inside of the door. When the door was closed, the X was on the inside, so he was not collected for execution the next morning. He was subsequently released.

Orient Express

Four men are sitting together at a table in the dining car of a train. All of them are starving. The waiter sets a plate with five small lamb chops on their table. After having eaten one each, they are all drooling for the last one, but cannot bring themselves to take it. The train enters a tunnel. In the dark there is a scream. As the train exits the tunnel, on the lamb chop there is a man's hand, with three forks solidly planted in it.

Ouch, That Hurts!

The woman was driving her car alone at night. She felt drowsy and was concerned about falling asleep at the wheel. She trapped the ends of her long hair in the window. There was no discomfort if she kept her head up, but if she nodded off and her head slumped, the painful tug on her hair would wake her up.

Perception of Deception

During World War II in England, if a member of a family was a vegetarian, the family was entitled to an extra cheese ration. Many families registered a child as a vegetarian to qualify for the extra cheese, which was shared among the children.

Plane Speaking

The child advised them not to paint the plane.

Pointless Exercise

His bathroom was being remodeled. He joined the local gym so he could take a shower.

Puppy Love

The bag stolen by the thief contained the dog's droppings.

Pushing the Envelope

The house he lived in was on the corner of two streets. He had lived there many years, but had recently installed an entrance on the second street, thus giving the house a second address. He had told only one person about this, so he could guess who had sent the letter when he saw it carried the new address.

Putt Out

The golfer was pleased that he had won the match. He raised his putter high in the air to acknowledge the applause of the watching crowd and was struck by lightning.

Reversal of Fortune

Oil is pumped from Kuwait to the Persian Gulf via a large pipeline. After the Gulf War, the pipeline flow was reversed to carry water in the other direction to extinguish the oil fires.

Road to Perdition

The road was the sixth road off Route 66 and was designated 666. Due to superstition, it was built as a short dead end.

Rolling Stone

The Rosetta stone bore the proclamation in two languages: Greek, which was well understood, and ancient Egyptian hieroglyphics, a language that had been lost. There were many Egyptian texts containing hieroglyphics and no one had been able to understand them. The Rosetta stone made it possible to decipher the hieroglyphics and unlock the secrets of the ancient Egyptians.

Seals on Strike

There was a group of nuns dressed in black and white in the front row of the audience. It is thought that the seals saw their shapes and mistook them for killer whales, which eat seals. The seals swam away in terror.

Shapely Object

It is a standard soccer field.

Smart Move

He was 60 years old and about to start drawing his pension annuity. Because smokers have a shorter life expectancy than non-smokers, they get higher annuity rates for the same lump sum. By smoking for a few months, he was able to claim he was a smoker and get a higher pension. He then gave up cigarettes. Smart move.

Spot the Dot

In words such as naïve, where the *i* must have two dots over it.

Stick with It

The man moistens the adhesive on the flap of the envelope and glues the stamp with it.

Stir the Porridge

The man visited his identical twin brother in prison. The brother persuaded him to trade places for a day but the convict brother did not return. His wrongdoing was discovered and both brothers ended up in the prison.

Stone Me

The man was leaving Antarctica, taking a pebble with him. It is absolutely forbidden by international treaty to take any material from Antarctica.

Stranded

The man was struck by a car that skidded onto a traffic island.

Suddenly Drowning

The man suffered from multiple personality disorder. While swimming, he underwent a personality change and became someone who did not know how to swim. He had to be rescued.

Tap, Tap, Tap

According to a well-known urban legend, a family from England drove to Spain for a vacation. While they were there, the grandmother who was with them died. Rather than bury her in Spain, they decided to take her body back to England. They wrapped it carefully and put it on the roof rack of the car. They stopped at a service station, where a thief stole the car. He heard a tapping from one of the ropes on the roof, so he stopped the car and unwrapped the bundle on the roof. He found himself staring at the face of the dead old woman.

Terse Verse

The piece is performed as a duet.

The Banal Canal

The company wanted to open a casino on its property but state laws were very restrictive regarding gambling. They took advantage of an old law that allowed gambling on steamboats on the Mississippi River and its tributaries by creating their own tributary on their land.

The Diver and the Ruler

The diver was a scuba diver on a diving boat in Sharm el Sheikh on the Red Sea in Egypt. Normally it would take an hour to reach the dive site, but the president of Egypt was staying at his villa on the coast. He had decreed that all vessels must observe a one-mile exclusion area around his villa. This was to reduce the risk of terrorist attack. All his predecessors had been assassinated and he wanted a normal death.

The Dog, the Cat, and the Canary

The man was a Muslim and he had three wives.

The Extra Shoe

The man was the Russian leader Nikita Khrushchev. At a heated meeting at the UN, he appeared to take off a shoe and bang the table with it in a display of temper. It was a prepared act—he had taken an extra shoe with him for that purpose.

The Find

Augusta wrote a book on a scholarly subject. It had been published and there was a copy in the university library. Augusta was eager to see if it had found readers, so she had placed a dollar bill in it, thinking that anyone who so much as took a cursory glance through the book would find and take the banknote. But when she saw that the banknote was still there after several months, it was all too obvious that no one had any interest in her book. Which made her sad, of course.

The Headless Nails

The battle of Waterloo in 1815 was a very close affair. At one point, the French cavalry under Marshal Ney overran the British guns in the center of Wellington's position. They usually carried headless nails with them to spike enemy guns. The nails were hammered into the fuse holes of the cannons to make them unusable. But the men with the nails had been killed in the attack and no nails could be found. The British cavalry then drove the French back. When Napoleon's Old Guard infantry launched their big attack, the British guns were used with deadly effect, and Napoleon was lost.

The Helpful Robber

Marjorie Halcrow Erskine of Chirnside, Scotland, apparently died in 1674. She was buried in a shallow grave by a sexton who was intent upon returning later to steal her jewelry. While the thieving sexton was trying to cut off her finger to appropriate a ring, she awoke. In her additional years of life following the burial, she went on to give birth to and raise two sons. No one knows what happened to the sexton.

The Ideal Candidate

The man chose the only candidate who was a smoker. He reasoned that if the man were prepared to risk his life smoking, he would probably be prepared to risk it to defend his employer.

The Kangaroo and the Emu

The kangaroo and the emu are unable to take a step back.

The Monarch's Secret

She used black blotting paper to blot her black ink so any image it left would be invisible.

The Queen's Mistake

It was an oversight on Queen Victoria's part that led to Berwick's being famously at war with Russia. The town was mentioned specifically in royal proclamations from the time of its annexation from Scotland. When Queen Victoria signed the declaration of war against Russia at the outbreak of the Crimean War in 1854, she did so with her full title: Victoria, Queen of Great Britain, Ireland, Berwick-upon-Tweed, and the British Dominions beyond the sea. When she signed the Paris Peace Treaty, however, Berwick was not mentioned. The issue of Berwick's being at war with Russia became a cause célèbre. It was resolved in the 1960s when a Russian diplomat visited and solemnly shook the mayor's hand. They agreed that the war was over. Thereafter, the Russians slept peacefully in their beds without worry about being attacked in the night by the Berwickers.

The Scratched Man

The man was the world's champion fisherman, fishing on a little island in a lake. His deadly rival, the world's second best fisherman, was on the shore, seething with envy. He poisoned the hook at the end of his line and, with a mighty and accurate cast (these guys can do it!), scratched his rival on the cheek with the deadly poison. He then reeled in his line, leaving his rival dead with only a little scratch on his cheek.

The Shine Sign

The shoeshine boy put up a notice saying One Shoe Shined Free.

The Stranger Who Sang

Peter was in a music shop that featured a bulletin board carrying advertisements related to musicians and music. He noticed the stranger reading the signs and asked him what he was interested in. One thing led to another and a new singer was recruited.

The Thoughtless Thief

The man took in a roll of film to be developed. But when the shopkeeper turned around, the man grabbed an expensive camera and ran out. When his film was developed some time later, it revealed an image of him standing outside his house.

Trapped

In the movie *The Sound of Music*, there appears a box of fruit marked "from Israel." The nation did not exist at the time of the Second World War, during which the movie is set.

Two Lefts Don't Make a Right

He is a baseball player who has just completed a home run.

Upstairs, Downstairs

The three clocks upstairs were mechanical (wind-up) clocks. The three clocks downstairs were digital electric clocks. There had been a very short power outage in the night. It had happened at 12:35 A.M., at which time the electric clocks reset to 12:00.

West Wing

The Vice President wrote back to the couple saying that he shared their concern regarding threats to all endangered wildlife in the United States. They were furious because the Texas Eagle was an Air Force service threatened with closure.

What a Drag

She was in training for a trip across the Antarctic, where she would have to pull a heavy sled across the snow and ice.

What Was the Point?

The Romans made spears with heads that came off on impact so that, in battle, their enemies could not pick up the spears and throw them back at the Romans.

Wheel of Fortune

The woman had been gambling for a while and losing, and she was down to her last $100. "Why not bet it on your age?" said a man sitting next to her. He went away but returned a short time later when he heard a commotion. He saw that the woman had collapsed and asked the croupier what had happened. "I don't know," replied the croupier. "She bet $100 on 29, and then, when 35 came up, she fainted."

Wind-up

It was a sundial.

Index